When Lt. Uhura's adorable pet tribble shows an incredible capacity to breed, it and its thousands and thousands of offspring take over practically every available inch of space on the Starship *Enterprise*.

And with each passing day, the *Enterprise* begins to more closely resemble a maternity ward than a spaceship.

What at first is considered a minor inconvenience soon becomes a galactic crisis as Captain Kirk and his crew discover...

**THE TROUBLE
WITH TRIBBLES**

OTHER **STAR TREK FOTONOVELS**™
YOU WILL ENJOY—

THE CITY ON THE
EDGE OF FOREVER

WHERE NO MAN
HAS GONE BEFORE

STAR TREK ™*

THE TROUBLE WITH TRIBBLES

written by **DAVID GERROLD**

adapted from the television series
created by **GENE RODDENBERRY**

THE TROUBLE WITH TRIBBLES
A Bantam Book / December 1977

Bantam Books are published by Bantam Books, Inc. Its trade-
mark, consisting of the words "Bantam Books" and the por-
trayal of a bantam, is registered in the United States Patent
Office and in other countries. Marca Registrada. Bantam
Books, Inc., 666 Fifth Avenue, New York, New York 10019.

PRINTED IN THE UNITED STATES OF AMERICA

0 9 8 7 6 5 4 3 2 1

A CONVERSATION WITH SCOTTY

by Caryl Eagle

*When faced with a temperamental tape recorder that just won't work, who would you rather be interviewing than **James Doohan,** also known as Lieutenant Commander Scott, Chief Engineer of the U.S.S.* Enterprise? *True to his character, he had it working in a moment, naturally eliciting this opening question:*

C.E.: How much of Scotty *is* Jim Doohan?

J.D.: I've always been interested in aviation and space technology. I've visited several NASA installations and if they called me tomorrow to go on the first space shuttle, I could be packed in fifteen minutes. When we started filming Star Trek, I began keeping notes and eventually gave Gene Roddenberry a 15 page journal explaining how everything aboard the Starship worked.

C.E.: Well, then, maybe you could explain the calculation of the various Stardates.

J.D.: Sorry—even Scotty couldn't figure out how those worked!

C.E.: Speaking of work, you certainly got quite a workout in *The Trouble With Tribbles.*

J.D.: Actually,that was my own doing. After they hired a stunt man, and I was sure he'd be paid, I told them I wanted to do the fight scene myself. I ended up doing about 95% of my own stunts. I had forgotten about that until I looked over your book. The reproductions are beautiful. I think the whole idea is fabulous. There's only one problem as far as I can see.

C.E.: Problem?

J.D.: Think about how many I'm going to have to autograph at all the Star Trek conventions!

(More about James Doohan and the conventions in our next book.)

CAST LIST

James T. Kirk, Captain
William Shatner

A man in his mid 30's whose independent nature and compassionate heart make him a natural leader. His overriding concern is always the well-being of his ship and crew.

Spock, First Officer
Leonard Nimoy

Chief Science Officer.
Of Vulcan and Terran heritage, which accounts for his analytical mind and extraordinary strength. His life is almost totally ruled by reason and logic.

Leonard McCoy, M.D., Lt. Commander
DeForest Kelley

Senior Ship's Surgeon, Head of Life Sciences Department. Though surrounded by the most advanced equipment the 24th century can offer, he still practices medicine more with his heart than his head.

Montgomery Scott, Lt. Commander
James Doohan

Chief Engineer.
A middle-aged man of Scottish descent whose knowledge of the ship's engineering section is boundless.

Pavel Chekov, Ensign
Walter Koenig

Ship's navigator who's fierce pride in his Russian heritage occasionally colors his views and opinions.

Cyrano Jones
Stanley Adams
An asteroid prospector and trader who travels through space not actually breaking the law, but occasionally bending it severely.

Nilz Baris
William Schallert
The rather pompous Federation's Undersecretary in charge of Agricultural Affairs for a quadrant of the Galaxy.

Uhura, Lt. Communications Officer
Nichelle Nichols

Koloth
William Campbell
Captain of a Klingon warship.

Mr. Lurry
White Bissel
Manager of Space Station K-7.

Korax
Michael Pataki
A Klingon; Captain Koloth's aide.

Admiral Fitzpatrick
Ed Riemers

Trader/Bartender
Guy Raymond

Ensign Freeman
Paul Baxley

Guard
David L. Ross

Arne Darvin
Charlie Brill
Assistant to Nilz Baris.

SPACE:

THE FINAL FRONTIER

THESE ARE THE VOYAGES OF
THE STARSHIP "ENTERPRISE".
ITS FIVE YEAR MISSION:
TO EXPLORE STRANGE NEW
WORLDS . . . TO SEEK OUT NEW
LIFE AND NEW CIVILIZA-
TIONS . . . TO BOLDLY GO
WHERE NO MAN HAS
GONE BEFORE.

THE TROUBLE
WITH TRIBBLES

CAPTAIN'S LOG:

STARDATE 4523.2

OUR PATH IS TAKING US INTO A QUADRANT
OF THE GALAXY THAT HAS BEEN UNDER
DISPUTE BETWEEN THE KLINGONS AND
THE FEDERATION SINCE INITIAL
CONTACT. THE BATTLE OF DONATU V WAS
FOUGHT NEAR HERE 23 SOLAR YEARS AGO.
THE RESULTS WERE INCONCLUSIVE. WE
ARE PRESENTLY APPROACHING DEEP
SPACE STATION K-7 WHICH IS NOW
WITHIN SENSOR RANGE.

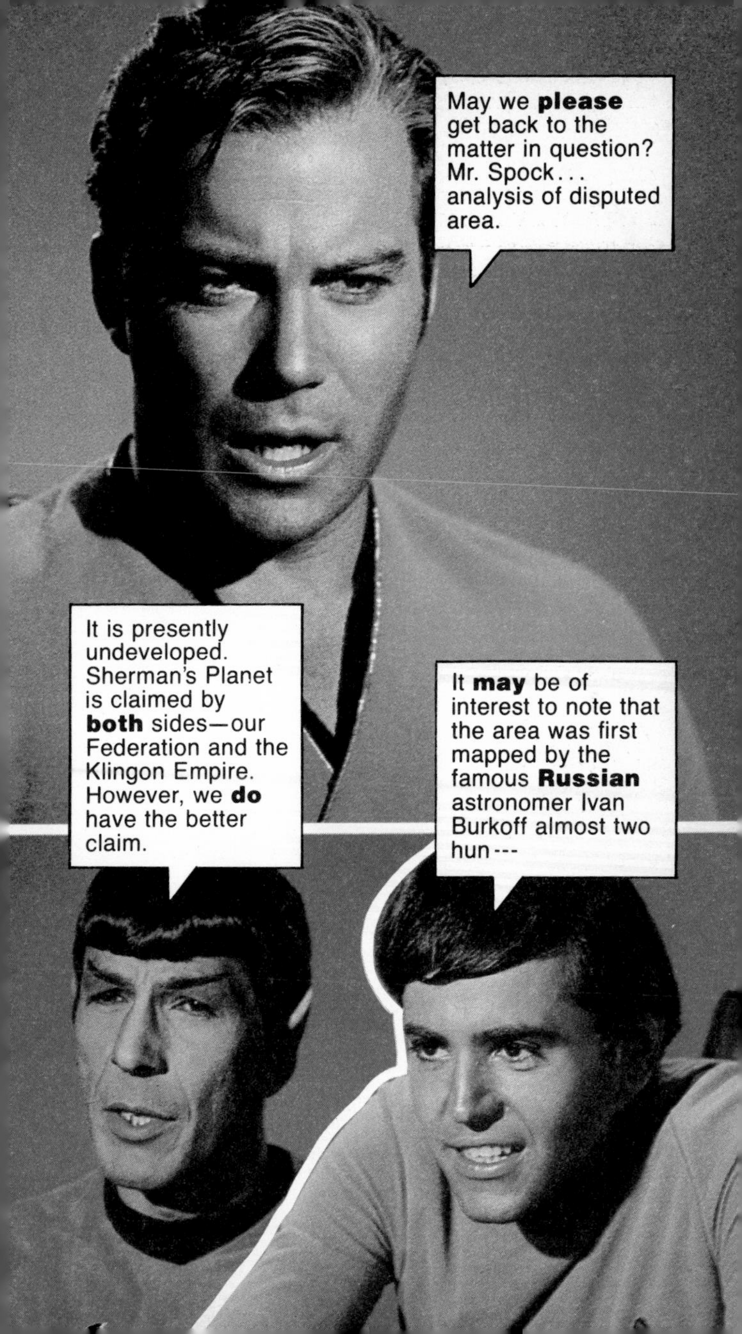
May we **please** get back to the matter in question? Mr. Spock . . . analysis of disputed area.
It is presently undeveloped. Sherman's Planet is claimed by **both** sides—our Federation and the Klingon Empire. However, we **do** have the better claim.
It **may** be of interest to note that the area was first mapped by the famous **Russian** astronomer Ivan Burkoff almost two hun---

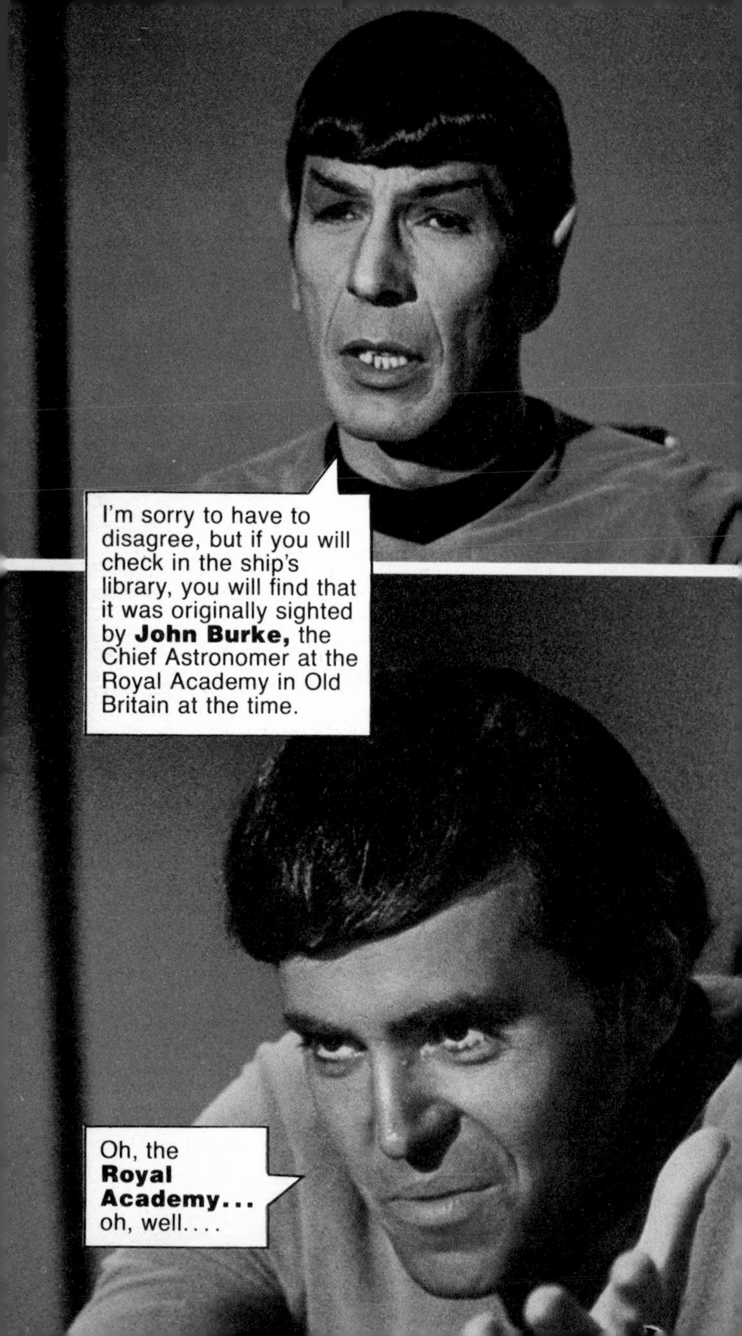
I'm sorry to have to disagree, but if you will check in the ship's library, you will find that it was originally sighted by **John Burke,** the Chief Astronomer at the Royal Academy in Old Britain at the time.
Oh, the **Royal Academy...** oh, well....

I hope the **rest** of your history isn't that faulty, Ensign. Now then. . . key points of dispute?
Under the terms of the **Organian Peace Treaty,** one side or the other must prove it can develop the planet **most efficiently.**
And, unfortunately, though the Klingons are **brutal** and **aggressive,** they are **most efficient.**

Before they can continue their discussion, though, the viewscreen on the table begins transmitting.
Captain—
Kirk here.
Captain, I'm picking up a subspace distress call . . . **priority channel.** It's from **space station K-7.**

Red Alert. Go to warp factor 6. Kirk out. Come on, let's get to the bridge.
This is a RED ALERT. All hands man your battle stations!

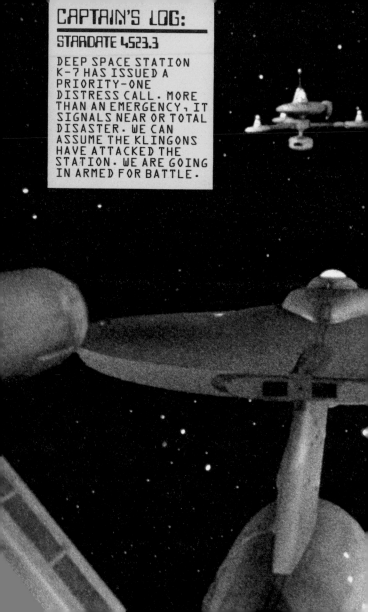

CAPTAIN'S LOG:

STARDATE 4523.3

DEEP SPACE STATION
K-7 HAS ISSUED A
PRIORITY-ONE
DISTRESS CALL. MORE
THAN AN EMERGENCY, IT
SIGNALS NEAR OR TOTAL
DISASTER. WE CAN
ASSUME THE KLINGONS
HAVE ATTACKED THE
STATION. WE ARE GOING
IN ARMED FOR BATTLE.

Priority-one distress call and it's **absolutely peaceful.** What's going on?
Lt. Uhura, break subspace silence.
Aye, sir. Channel's open.
Space station K-7—this is Captain Kirk of the U.S.S. *Enterprise.* **State the nature of your emergency.**
Captain Kirk, this is Mr. Lurry, manager of K-7. I must **apologize** for the distress call.

Captain Kirk, this is Nilz Baris. He's out from Earth to take charge of the Development Project for Sherman's Planet.

And this is my assistant, Arne Darvin.

This is my First Officer, Mr. Spock.

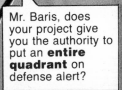

Mr. Baris, does your project give you the authority to put an **entire quadrant** on defense alert?

Mr. Baris is the Federation Under-Secretary in charge of Agricultural Affairs in this quadrant.

And **that,** Captain, **does** give him the authority.
Now, Captain, I want you to beam down **all** available security guards from your ship and post them around the storage compartments.

Storage compartments?. . . **Storage compartments?**
The storage compartments containing the **quadro-triticale.**

Quadro-triticale is not **just** wheat, Captain. Of course, I wouldn't expect you or Mr. Spock to know about such things, but quadro-triticale is a rather—

Quadro-triticale is a high-yield grain. A four lobed hybrid of wheat and rye. A perennial also, if I'm not mistaken. Its root grain, triticale, can trace its ancestry all the way back to Twentieth Century Canada where---

Uh...Mr. Spock, you've made your point!

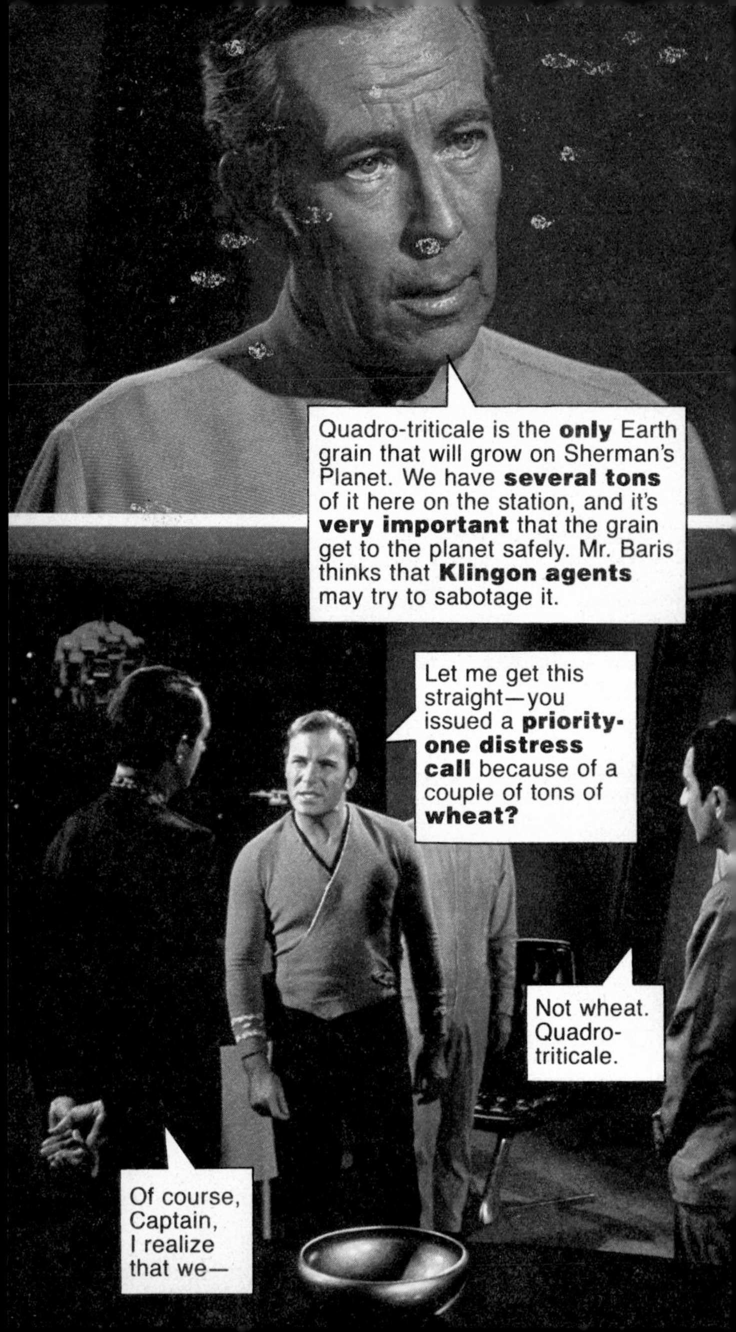
Quadro-triticale is the **only** Earth grain that will grow on Sherman's Planet. We have **several tons** of it here on the station, and it's **very important** that the grain get to the planet safely. Mr. Baris thinks that **Klingon agents** may try to sabotage it.
Let me get this straight—you issued a **priority-one distress call** because of a couple of tons of **wheat?**
Not wheat. Quadro-triticale.
Of course, Captain, I realize that we—

Mr. Baris, you summoned the *Enterprise* **without** an emergency. You'll take **full responsibility** for it.
Misuse of the priority-one channel is a Federation offense.
I did **not** misuse the priority-one channel. I **want** that grain protected.

Captain, couldn't you at least post a couple of guards? We do have a large number of ships passing through the space station and I have no extra personnel available.

And you think **I** do?
First my ship is put on alert by some **phoney emergency call** and now my crew is supposed to **rush** down here to guard some **wheat?**
May I suggest, Captain, that it would seem a **logical precaution.** The Sherman's Planet affair is of **extreme importance** to the Federation.
Reluctantly, Kirk agrees and contacts the Enterprise.
Lt. Uhura, secure from general quarters and beam down **two** and **only two** security guards. Have them report to Mr. Lurry. Then authorize shore leave for all off-duty personnel.
Yes, Captain.

Captain Kirk! How **dare** you authorize a mere **two** men for a project of this importance? Star Fleet Command is going to—
Mr. Baris, I have **never** questioned the orders or the intelligence of any representative of the Federation. That is . . . **until now.**

Later, in the space station's bar, Kirk is still seething over the day's events.

Summoning a starship on a priority A-1 channel to guard some **storage compartments**? Can you **believe** that?

Nevertheless, Captain, the Klingons would **not** enjoy seeing us successfully develop Sherman's Planet.

Well, well, well, look who's here! What a shame, we were just leaving. I see you didn't waste any time taking your shore leave.

The bar seems to be a very popular gathering spot for Starship personnel.

Certainly not! How often do **I** get shore leave?

Lt. Uhura asked me to come along and help her shop.

One second, Mr. Chekov. What do you make of **this?**
Oh, **quadro-triticale.** I've **read** about this, but I've never **seen** any before. It's a **Russian** hybrid developed by Ivan---
Forget I even **mentioned** it!
Does **everybody** know about this wheat but **me?**

Moving to the bar, Uhura and Chekov overhear the bartender who is engaged in some kind of business deal with a rather disreputable looking peddler.

I told you **before,** Mr. Jones, and I'm telling you **again.** I **don't** want any more Spican Flame Gems. Thanks to **you, I already** have enough to last me a **lifetime.**

How **sad** for you, my friend. You won't find a finer stone **anywhere.**

But never matter. I have something even **better.**

Surely you would want some Antarian Glow Water.
Why would I? I use **that** to polish the Flame Gems!
You're a difficult man to reach. But I have something from the **far reaches** of the galaxy!

Surely you would like some of **these.**
Possibly. It depends on **how much** you want.

Why, it's **alive.** I've never seen one of those before. Do you mind if I hold it for a second?
Why, of **course** not, my dear!

Oh…it's **adorable.** What is it?

It's a **tribble.** Without a doubt, the **sweetest** creature known to man… excepting, of course, **your** lovely self.
Oh, it's **purring.** Listen, the sweet little thing is **actually purring!**
It's only saying that it likes you.

I'd just **love** to have one as a pet. Are you selling them?
That's what we're trying to decide right now. Mr. Jones, I'll give you **one credit** apiece.
My friend, a more reasonable price would be **ten credits** apiece. You can see for yourself how much the lovely lady appreciates the **finer things** in life.

He won't bite... will he?

Sir! Transporting harmful animals from one planet to another is **against regulations.** Or weren't you aware of that? Besides, tribbles have no teeth.

I wish you two gentlemen would come to some decision because **I'd** like to buy one. I think he's **sweet**.

All right! I'll **double** my offer. **Two credits.**

No deal.

Three credits?

You must be **joking!**

You're talking yourself out of a deal, friend. My last and **final** offer is six credits. Not a credit more. **Take it or leave it.**
All right, you robber. Six credits.

Now then, what are **you** selling them for?

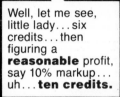

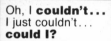

You're **wrong,** my dear friend. There will be **no charge** for **this** tribble. It happens to be my **sample** and I'll do with it as I **please.** And, I please to **give** it to the lovely little lady here.

Oh, I **couldn't...** I just couldn't... **could I?**

What are you trying to do? **Ruin the market?**
Trust me. Once the lovely lady starts to show that precious little darling around, you won't be able to **keep up** with them.
For that matter, ***no one*** *will!*

The following day, as the Starship maintains its position off space station K-7, Captain Kirk and Spock are in the Briefing Room discussing the situation.

I have heard what you said, Captain. Nevertheless, I see **no alternative.**

Our responsibilities are **quite clear** and---

Message from Star Fleet, Captain. Priority Channel. It's Admiral Fitzpatrick. I'm putting him on visual.

Captain Kirk here, Admiral Fitzpatrick.

Captain, it is not necessary to remind you of the **importance** to the Federation of Sherman's Planet. The **key** to our winning of this planet is the grain quadro-triticale. The shipment of it **must** be protected.

Effective immediately you will render any aid and assistance which Under-Secretary Baris may require. The safety of the grain and the project is **your** responsibility. Star Fleet out!

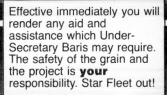

Once again they are interrupted.

Captain Kirk! Sensors are picking up a **Klingon battle cruiser** that is rapidly closing in on the space station.

Call a **Red Alert** and get Mr. Lurry on the bridge's viewscreen! **We'll be right up!** Kirk out.

Mr. Lurry! There's a **Klingon war ship** hanging one hundred kilometers off your station!

Captain Kirk, I **don't** think the Klingons are planning to attack us.

Why **not?**

CAPTAIN'S LOG:

STARDATE 4524.2

A KLINGON WARSHIP IS HOVERING ONLY A HUNDRED KILOMETERS FROM DEEP SPACE STATION K-7, WHILE ITS CAPTAIN WAITS IN THE STATION MANAGER'S OFFICE. SPOCK AND I ARE BEAMING DOWN.

The room is filled with tension and mutual distrust as the two captains, representing opposing forces in the galaxy, come face to face.

Ah, my **dear** Captain Kirk.

My **dear** Captain Koloth. What brings you to K-7?

Let me **assure** you that my intentions are **peaceful.** As I've already told Mr. Lurry, the purpose of my presence here is to invoke shore leave rights.
Shore leave rights?
Captain, we Klingons are not as luxury-minded as you Earthers. We do not equip our ships with . . . how shall I say it? . . . **non-essentials.**

We have been in space for **five months** and what we choose as recreation is our **own** business.

I might also add that under the terms of the Organian Peace Treaty, you **cannot** refuse us.

Captain, may I speak to you a minute?

Yes, well... **I** don't make those decisions. **Mr. Lurry** is in charge of those matters.

Kirk, I don't want them here, but I don't have the authority to refuse.
Hmmm. . . Well, **I** have the authority to act and I'm **going** to use it.
My **dear** Captain Koloth, you may indeed bring your men down on shore leave. **But only 12 at a time.** And I assure you that for every man you bring here, I shall have one security guard. **There will be no trouble.**
Captain Kirk, there's been no **formal** declaration of hostilities between our two respective governments. So, **naturally,** our relationship **will** be a peaceful one.

Let us **both** take steps to **keep** it that way.

Spock, I may be repeating myself, but let's get back to the ship.

Anxious for a few minutes of relaxation, Kirk and Spock join several of the crew in the Starship's Recreation Room.

Ah, Scotty, what are you doing? Reading **another** technical journal? Don't you ever **relax?**

But Captain, I **am** relaxing.

Oh, **Captain!** Well, I hadn't **intended** to sir, but... eh... the tribbles had **other** plans!
With amazement and amusement, Kirk watches as Spock cuddles one of the baby tribbles with almost... ***tenderness?***
A **most curious** creature, Captain. It's trilling seems to have a **tranquilizing effect** on the human nervous system. Fortunately, of course, **I** am **immune** to its effect.
So I **see,** Mr. Spock!

Well, all right, Doctor. But if you're going to **dissect** it, I don't want to know about it!
Lieutenant Uhura, do you mind if I take one of these down to the lab and see what makes it "tick"?
I won't harm a hair on its head... wherever **that** is.
Say, Lieutenant, seeing as you're giving them away, can **I** have one?
Oh sure. Why not? I think they're old enough. As a matter of fact, why don't you **all** take one?

As Kirk and Spock head back to the bridge...
Lt. Uhura is going to have her hands **full,** if that tribble ever has any **more** babies.
Bridge to Captain Kirk. Mr. Baris is waiting on Channel E to speak to you, sir.
Pipe it down here, will you, Mr. Chekov?
Aye, sir. Mr. Baris is coming on.

Kirk, this station is **swarming** with Klingons.
I was not aware, Mr. Baris, that **twelve** Klingons constitutes a **swarm.**

Captain Kirk, there are Klingon soldiers on this station. Now I want you to keep that grain **safe.**
Mr. Baris, I already **have** guards around the grain. I **also** have guards around the Klingons. The **only** reason those guards are there is because **Star Fleet** wants them there. As for what **you** want... It has been noted and logged. **Kirk out!!!**

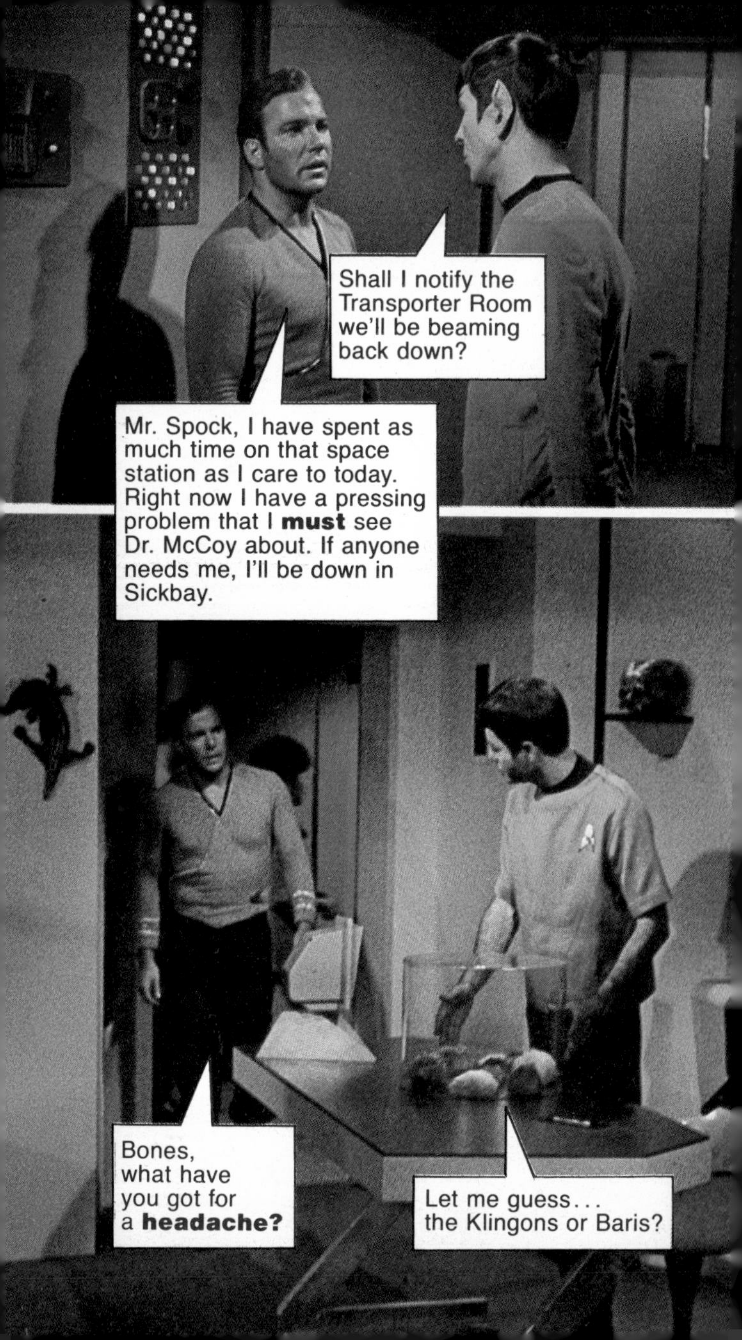

Shall I notify the Transporter Room we'll be beaming back down?
Mr. Spock, I have spent as much time on that space station as I care to today. Right now I have a pressing problem that I **must** see Dr. McCoy about. If anyone needs me, I'll be down in Sickbay.
Bones, what have you got for a **headache?**
Let me guess... the Klingons or Baris?

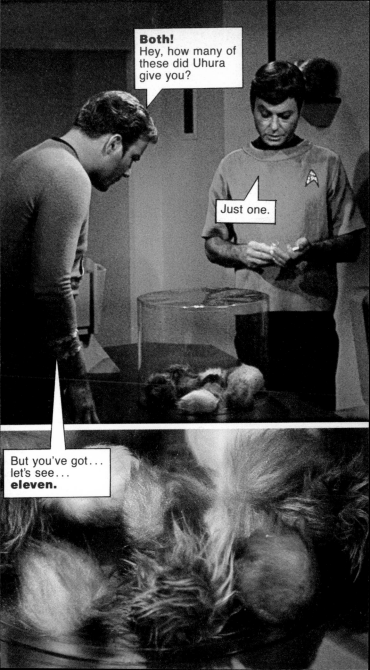

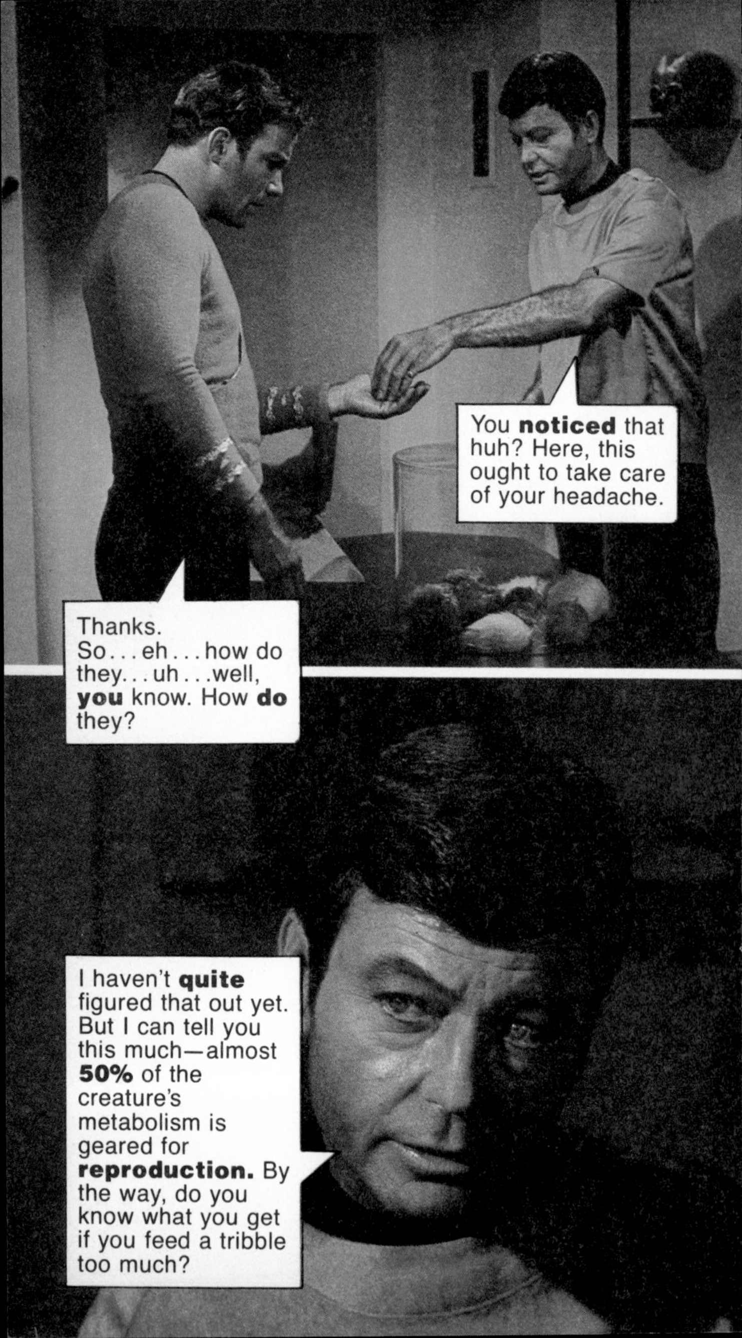
You **noticed** that huh? Here, this ought to take care of your headache.
Thanks. So . . . eh . . . how do they. . . uh . . .well, **you** know. How **do** they?
I haven't **quite** figured that out yet. But I can tell you this much—almost **50%** of the creature's metabolism is geared for **reproduction.** By the way, do you know what you get if you feed a tribble too much?

A **fat** tribble?

No! You get a whole bunch of **hungry** little tribbles.

Well, Bones, I wish I could help you, but all I can suggest is that you consider opening up a **maternity ward.**

Later that day, Kirk briefs several of his men who are about to go to K-7 on shore leave.

...and don't forget, avoid trouble with the Klingons **no matter what.** Mr. Scott, I want **you** to make sure that the men stay in groups.

Well, Captain, I wasn't planning on going myself.

Oh yes, you are! I need you down there to make sure that everybody stays out of trouble. Do you understand me, Scotty?

Yes, sir. **Certainly,** sir.

The group is beamed down to the space station for a pleasant evening of conversation and, perhaps, some **light refreshment.**

But they hadn't anticipated running into Cyrano Jones who, as always, is trying to promote a little business.

Ah, friends... Can I offer you a charming little tribble?

prrrrr
No, thanks. We have **several** on the Starship already.
Very well.
Undaunted, the irrepressible Mr. Jones moves on to the next table of prospective customers.

Perhaps one of **you** gents may be interested in making a **small purchase**...
My friend Klingon, how about a **harmless little tribble?** They **do** have such a calming purr.
*But as Cyrano moves the tribble nearer to the Klingon, a very **strange** thing happens—the Klingon reacts as if he is about to be attacked by a **vicious animal!***

Cyrano makes one last attempt.
Ah, my good friend, how would you like to enter, into another little transaction? This time, a tribble for a spot of --
A tribble? A tribble? I'm beginning to think there's no such thing as a tribble.

And from underneath his counter the bartender begins producing tribble after tribble after tribble!
Remember the cute little fellow you sold me the other day? Well it had a blessed event and then it had another and another....

Meanwhile, in another part of the room:
When are you going to get off that **milk diet,** lad?
This is vodka!
Where **I** come from, that's **soda pop.** Now, **scotch** is a drink for a **man.**
A drink for a **man?** Why, it was invented by a **little old lady** from Lenningrad!

Mr. Peddler, those Earthers **really like** those fuzzy things, don't they?

Approaching the bar for a refill, the Klingon officer makes sure to keep his distance from the tribbles.

Oh, **yes.** Tribbles are extremely popular. **Everybody**...eh... **most people** ... like them.

Well, **I** don't. But then, I don't like **Earthers** much either.

He may be a **swaggering, overbearing, tin-plated dictator** with delusions of **god-hood...** but he's **not** soft.
That's it! I will **not** allow you to speak of Captain Kirk in that manner!
Take it **easy,** lad. **Everybody's** entitled to an opinion.

But you **heard** what he called the Captain!

Of **course** he did. And **I** heard what **he** said. So, if I think that your Captain is a **Denebian Slime Devil,** well... that's **my** opinion.

Now you've gone **too far.**

Forget it, Ensign. It's not worth fighting for. We're big enough to take a few insults. Now **sit down** and finish your drink.

Of course, I'd say that Captain Kirk **deserves** his ship. We **all** like the *Enterprise.* We really do. Who **wouldn't** like a sagging old **rust bucket** that's designed like a **garbage scow?** Half the quadrant knows it. That's why they're learning to speak **Klingonese.**

With the Captain's words ringing in his ears, Scott tries valiantly to control his temper.

Laddy, don't you think you should **rephrase** that?

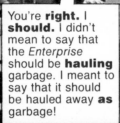

Taunted by the belligerent Klingon beyond his endurance, Scott is unable to restrain himself and...

...throws such a powerful punch at the Klingon's jaw that Korax is sent flying across the room!

Within seconds, both crews are on their feet and the underlying tension that has filled the room is given full rein and the brawl begins...

Two anxious spectators watch the entire slug-fest with avid interest and dramatically differing points of view.

Isn't **someone** going to stop them? This is **terrible.** They're going to break all my furniture.

They **are** getting rather violent, aren't they? But don't worry. I know where I can get you a **very good deal** on some new tables and chairs.

And the fight continues and continues and continues...until every last man is bruised, hurt and exhausted.

CAPTAIN'S LOG:

STARDATE 4525.6

A SMALL DISTURBANCE BETWEEN THE KLINGON CREW AND MEMBERS OF THE "ENTERPRISE" CREW HAS BROKEN OUT ABOARD SPACE STATION K-7. I AM FORCED TO CANCEL SHORE LEAVE FOR BOTH SHIPS.

Having assembled all crew members involved in the fracas, Kirk has spent the last several minutes in an unsuccessful attempt to find out how the whole thing began.

I don't know, sir? Is that **all** you men know how to say? Well, I'll give you some time to think of a more original answer. You're **all** confined to quarters until further notice. **Dismissed.** Except **you,** Scotty. I'm counting on you to tell me the **truth.**

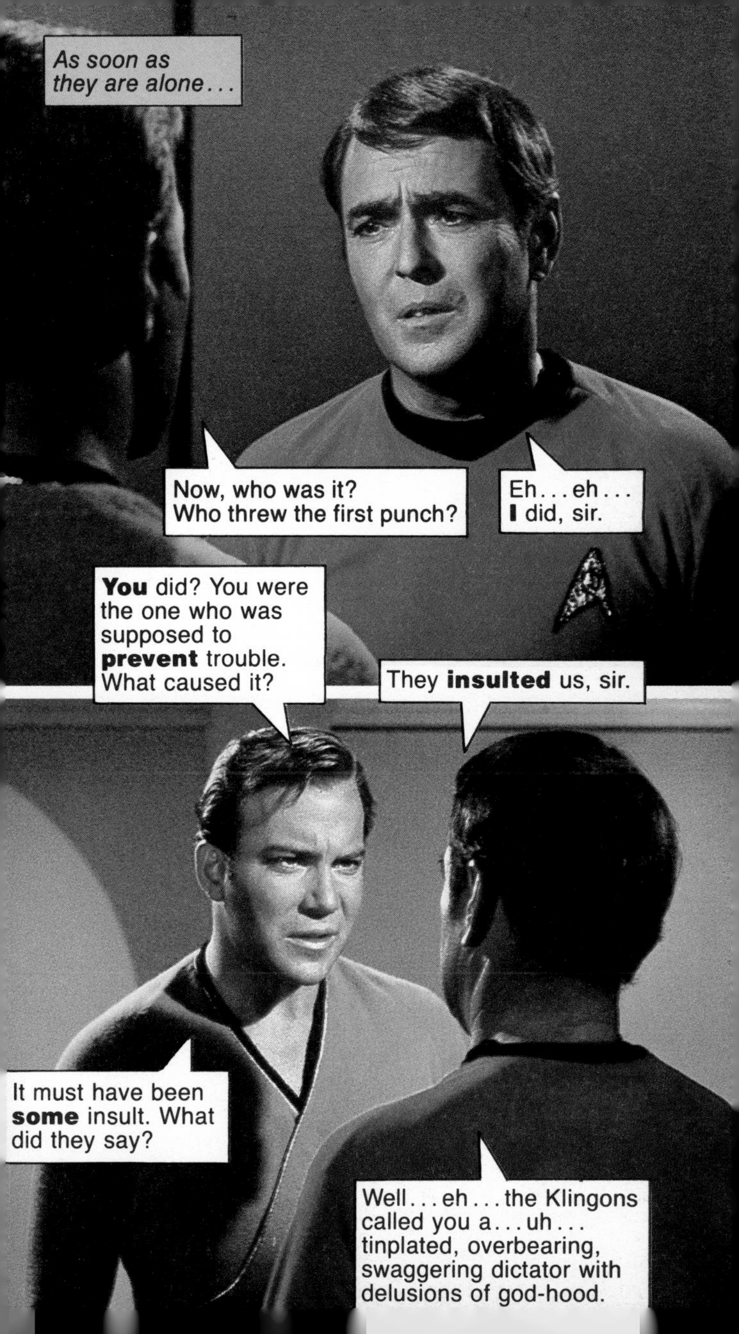
As soon as they are alone . . .
Now, who was it? Who threw the first punch?
Eh . . . eh . . . **I** did, sir.
You did? You were the one who was supposed to **prevent** trouble. What caused it?
They **insulted** us, sir.
It must have been **some** insult. What did they say?
Well . . . eh . . . the Klingons called you a . . . uh . . . tinplated, overbearing, swaggering dictator with delusions of god-hood.

Is that **all?**
No, sir. They also compared you with the Denebian Slime Devil and then they said you were a —

I get the picture, Scotty. So, after they said all this, that's when you hit the Klingons?
No, sir. I didn't.

You told us to avoid trouble and I didn't see that it was worth fighting about. After all, we're big enough to take a **few** insults, aren't we?

So what was it that made you start the fight?
It was when they called the *Enterprise* a **garbage scow,** sir. I **couldn't** let them get away with **that.**

I see...you hit the Klingons because they insulted the *Enterprise*, **not** because --

Well, sir, it was a matter of **pride.**

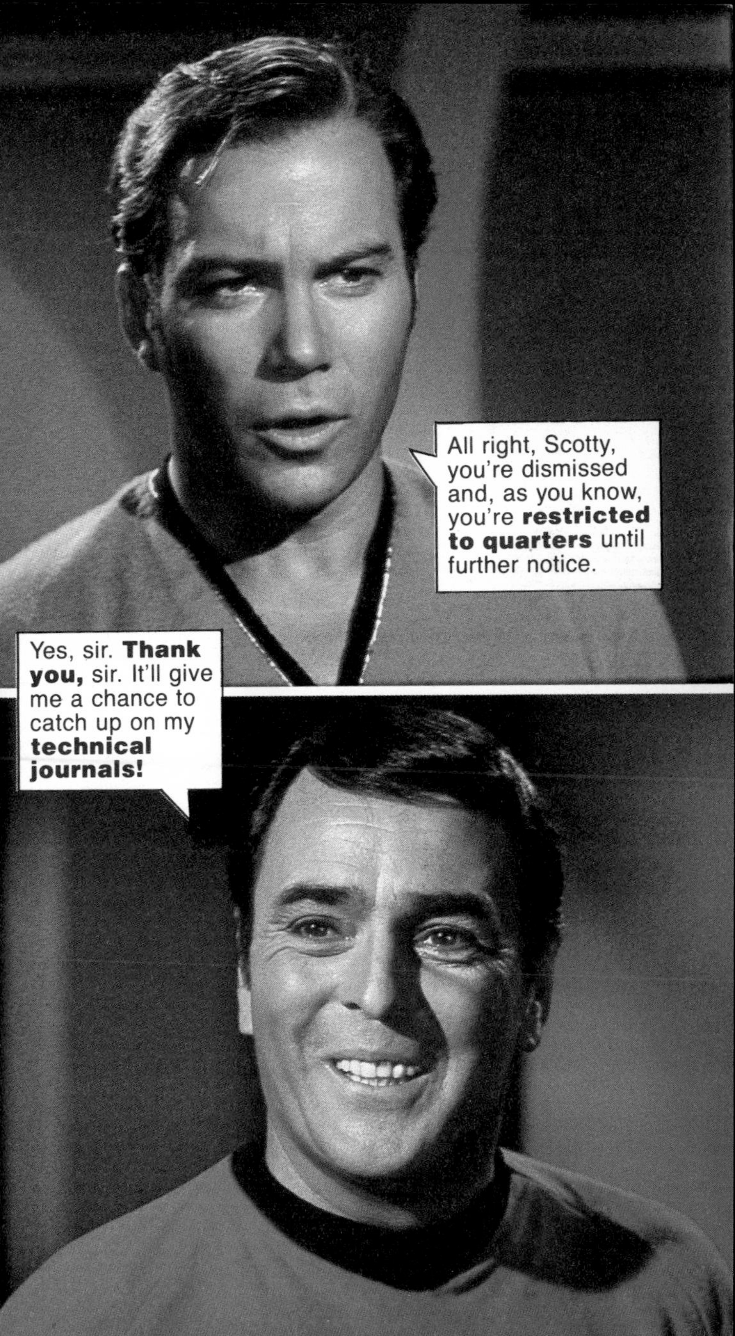
All right, Scotty, you're dismissed and, as you know, you're **restricted to quarters** until further notice.
Yes, sir. **Thank you,** sir. It'll give me a chance to catch up on my **technical journals!**

Dr. McCoy and Spock have been placed on special assignment by Captain Kirk to find out just what makes the tribbles propagate so abundantly. And all the time that they have been forced to spend together doing their research is beginning to wear away at their already tenuous relationship.
Why, Mr. Spock, you look **worried.** What's the matter?
There's something **disquieting** about these creatures.
Oh, don't tell me you've got a **feeling** about them.

Don't be **insulting,** Doctor. They remind me of the lilies of the field—"They toil not, neither do they spin." But they do seem to **eat** a great deal. I see no practical use for them.
Does **everything** have to have a practical use for you? Tribbles are nice and soft and furry and they also make a pleasant sound.
So would an **ermine violin,** Doctor, but I see no advantage in having one.

It is a **human characteristic** to love little animals. **Especially** if they are attractive in some way.

Doctor, I am well aware of human characteristics. I am frequently **inundated** by them, but I have trained myself to put up with practically **anything.**

Spock, I don't know too much about these little tribbles yet, but there is **one** thing I've discovered... I **like** them... better than I like **you.**

They do indeed have **one** redeeming characteristic, Doctor. They do not **talk** too much. Now, if you'll **excuse** me, sir....

As Captain Kirk enters the bridge that afternoon, he has more than the usual worries of a Starship Captain on his mind.

First Baris and his quadro-triticale and now the Klingons...**what next?** I really don't feel like tackling any more big problems for awhile.

That's **good.** Because Kirk's **next** problem isn't a very big one. In fact, it's quite **small**... and furry... and soft... and unfortunately has chosen Kirk's command chair as its nest.

What in the **world...?**

As he slowly surveys the bridge, the true extent of the tribbles' population explosion becomes painfully apparent...

What are we running here? A ship or a **wild life sanctuary?**

Lt. Uhura, how did all these tribbles get on the bridge?

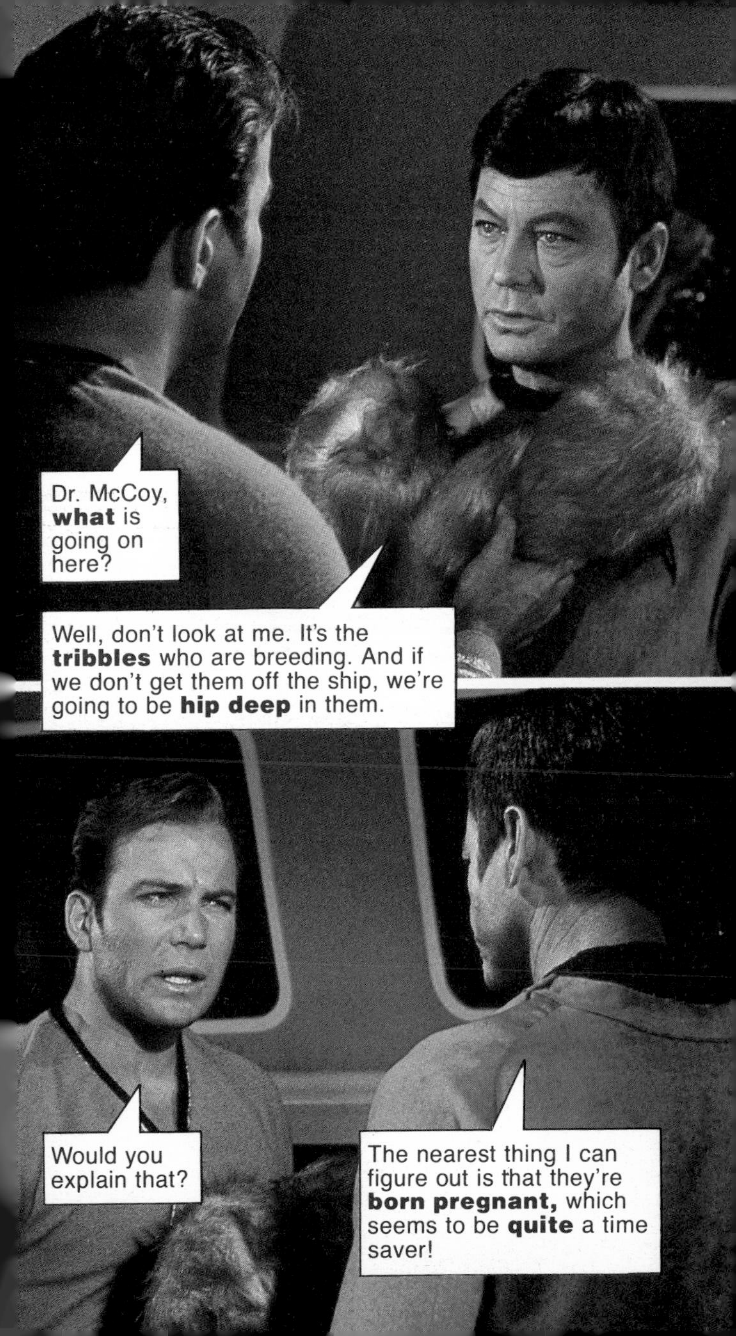
Dr. McCoy, **what** is going on here?
Well, don't look at me. It's the **tribbles** who are breeding. And if we don't get them off the ship, we're going to be **hip deep** in them.
Would you explain that?
The nearest thing I can figure out is that they're **born pregnant,** which seems to be **quite** a time saver!

I know, but **really!**

And, from my observations, it seems they're **bi-sexual**... reproducing at will. And **brother,** have they got a **lot** of will!

Captain, I am **forced** to agree with the Doctor. I've been running computations on their rate of reproduction. The figures are taking an **alarming** direction. They are consuming our supplies and returning **nothing.**

Oh, but they **do** give us something, Mr. Spock. They give us **love.** As a matter of fact, Cyrano Jones says that a tribble is the only love that money **can** buy.

But too much of **anything**, Lieutenant, even **love**, isn't necessarily a **good** thing.

Have the maintenance crew clean up the **entire** ship. And then contact Mr. Lurry and tell him I'm beaming down.

Aye-aye, sir.

Have him find Cyrano Jones and hold him. And, Lieutenant, get these tribbles **off** the bridge.

Yes, Captain.

But his discussion with the peddler proves less than successful.
Captain Kirk, I'm **mystified** at your tone of voice. I've done **nothing** to warrant such severe treatment.
Oh, **really?**
Surely you must have realized what would happen if you removed the tribbles from their predatory-filled environment into an environment where their natural multiplicative proclivities would have no restraining factors?
Why. . . eh . . . **of course** . . . ahh. . .what did you say?

By removing the tribbles from their natural habitat you have, so to speak, removed the cork from the bottle and allowed the genie to escape.

Well, if you mean that they **breed** quickly, you're absolutely right. That's how I maintain my stock. But breeding animals is **not** against regulations. Only breeding **dangerous** ones is. And tribbles are **certainly** not dangerous!

Just **incredibly** prolific!

Precisely. And at six credits a head, well, that is, **a body,** it mounts up. Now, even though its been **extremely** pleasant chatting with you, I really **must** be going.

One second, Mr. Jones. I was wondering if you've ever considered selling an **instruction** or **maintenance manual** with these things?

If I did, what would happen to man's search for knowledge? Well, I must be tending my ship. **Au revoir!**

As Cyrano leaves he passes the icy stares of Baris and Darvin.

Here he is, Mr. Secretary. You can talk to him now.

No, first I want to speak with Kirk.

Captain, I consider your security measures a **disgrace.** In **my** opinion, you have taken this **very important project** far too lightly.

On the **contrary,** sir. I think of this project as **very** important. It is **you** I take lightly!

I want you to know that I am going to report this **fully** to the proper authorities. You have given free and complete access to this station to a man who is quite probably a **Klingon agent!**
Now that's a **very serious** charge. To whom are you referring?

To whom am I referring? Why, to that man who just walked out of here.
Cyrano Jones? A Klingon agent?

Didn't you hear me?
He **heard** you. But he simply could not **believe** his ears. What evidence do you have against Mr. Jones?

My assistant here has kept Mr. Jones under **close surveillance** for quite some time. And his actions have been **most suspicious.** I believe he was involved in that little altercation between your men and the Klingons.

In addition, I checked his ship's log and it seems that he was within the Klingon sphere of influence less than four months ago.

The man is an **independent scout,** Captain. It's quite possible that he is **also** a Klingon spy.

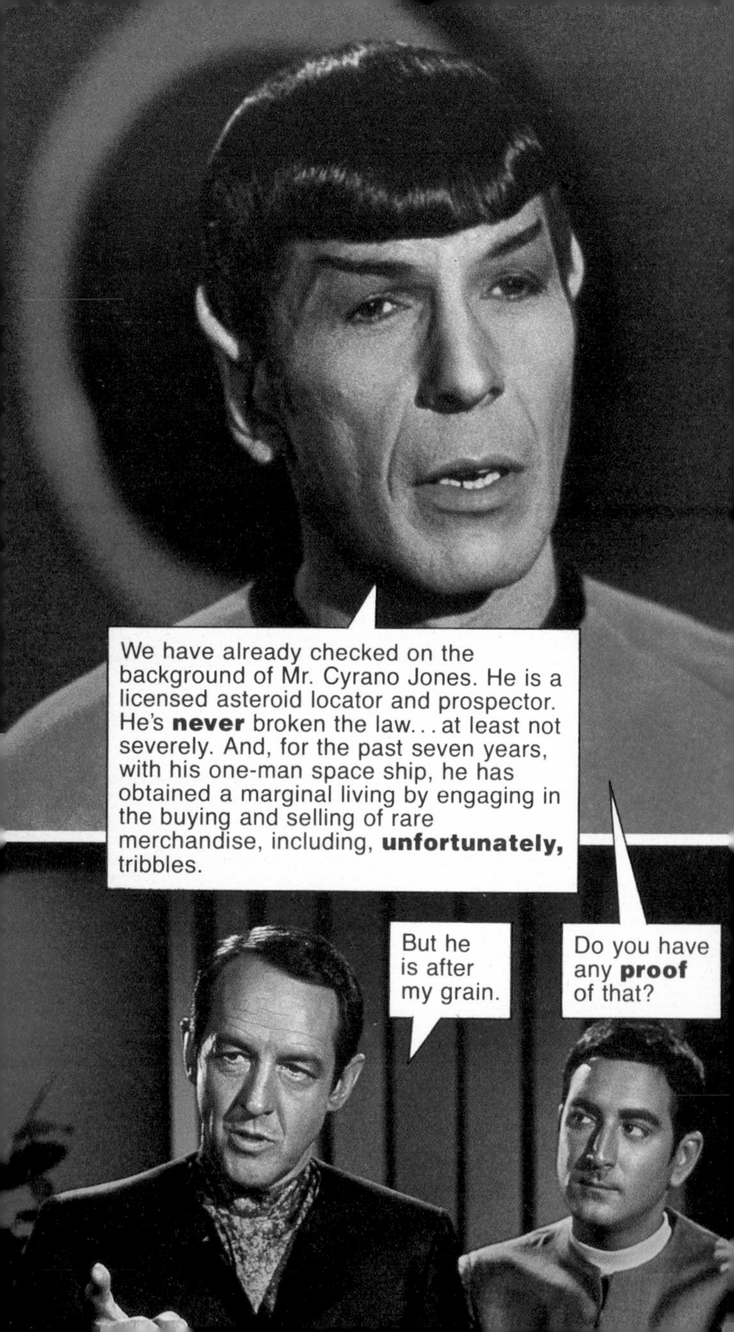
We have already checked on the background of Mr. Cyrano Jones. He is a licensed asteroid locator and prospector. He's **never** broken the law. . . at least not severely. And, for the past seven years, with his one-man space ship, he has obtained a marginal living by engaging in the buying and selling of rare merchandise, including, **unfortunately,** tribbles.
But he is after my grain.
Do you have any **proof** of that?

You **can't** deny that he has disrupted this station.

People have disrupted space stations before without being Klingon agents. **Sometimes** all they need is a **title,** Mr. Baris. Unfortunately, disrupting a space station is **not** an offense. Now, if you'll excuse me, I have a ship to tend to. **Au revoir!**

*The following day, all is relatively quiet on the Starship, except of course for the steady hum of the **darling** little tribbles.*

Entering the Recreation Room, Kirk immediately realizes that his orders concerning the tribbles have not been fully carried out.

I thought I made it **perfectly clear** that I wanted the maintenance crew to clear up the **entire** ship!

I believe they're **trying** to, Captain, but the tribbles are not exactly **cooperating.**

The point is dramatically demonstrated when Kirk has his lunch and finds that he is **sharing** it with several tribbles.

What is going **on** here?

Eh...Mr. Spock, would you care for a **cup of tribble?**
I think not, Captain.
Presumably, ***this*** *is the tribble that breaks the Captain's back!*
This is **all** I'm going to take! **I want these things off the ship!** I don't care if it takes every man and woman we've got! **I want them OFF the ship!!!**

Just then Scott passes by.

Scotty, what are you doing with all of those? The maintenance crew is going to clear them away.

I **know** that, but they've gotten into the **machinery** and they're probably in all the **food processors** too. They must have crawled through one of the air vents!

Captain, there are vents of that type on the space station.

And in the storage compartments!

A picture instantly formulates in Kirk's mind as he rushes over to the intercommunicator and contacts the bridge.

This is Kirk. Contact manager Lurry and Nilz Baris. Have them meet us near the storage compartments.

*Kirk and Spock are immediately transported down to the space station where they are met by two **very anxious** men.*
Where are you going? **What's wrong?**
Plenty, if what I **think** has happened **has** happened. **Follow me!**

The group hurries to the storage compartments containing the precious grain.
Guard, is that door secure?
Yes, sir. **Certainly,** sir. **Nothing** could get in.

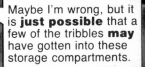

Maybe I'm wrong, but it is **just possible** that a few of the tribbles **may** have gotten into these storage compartments.

*But Kirk is wrong. A **few** of the tribbles **haven't** gotten in.*

A **whole bunch** of the tribbles have gotten in and within seconds a whole bunch get **out.**

Star Fleet Academy **never** prepared me for **this!**

Spock takes a closer look at one of the little invaders.

Captain, there's something **very wrong** with this tribble. Its body seems to be **gorged.**

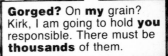

Gorged? On **my** grain? Kirk, I am going to hold **you** responsible. There must be **thousands** of them.

Hundreds of thousands!

1,771,561, to be a **bit** more precise. That's assuming one tribble multiplying with an average litter of ten and producing a new generation every twelve hours over a period of three days.

That's assuming that they got here **only** three days ago!
And allowing for the amount of grain consumed and the volume of the storage compartment.
Kirk, you should have **known.** You are **personally responsible** for turning the Development Project into a total **disaster!**

And I also want you to know that I am through being intimidated, Kirk. You have insulted me . . . ignored me . . . and walked all over me! You have abused your authority and you have rejected my requests. And this . . . THIS . . . is the result!

I am going to hold you responsible!
Mr. Baris, I'll hold you in irons if you don't shut up!

Something about the tribbles suddenly catches the Doctor's attention. But what is it? It's the **silence.** All those friendly tribbles and no noise? No soft purring hum?
Jim, this tribble is **dead.**
You're **right,** Doctor. So is **this** one.
A quick reading on his scanner confirms his suspicions.
Quite a **lot** of them are dead! **Some** are still alive, but they won't be for long.
A **logical** assumption is that there is something in the grain.

Bones! I want the tribbles, the grain, **everything,** analyzed. I want to know what killed these tribbles!
I haven't even figured out what keeps them **alive** yet. All right, I'll get to work on it **right away.** If I find out anything, I'll let you know.

That isn't going to do you any good, Kirk. This project is **ruined** and Star Fleet is going to hear about it. And when they do, they will have a **Board of Inquiry** and they will **roast you alive!** And I'm going to be there, Kirk, to enjoy **every minute** of it!

Well, until that Board of Inquiry convenes, I'm **still** a Captain.

And as Captain, I want **two things** done. First, find Cyrano Jones, and second... **close that hatch!**

I'm afraid it is necessary, Mr. Jones. I have a few questions that I need to ask you. Please sit down.

But before the questioning can begin, they are interrupted by Captain Koloth and his aide.

Captain Kirk! I am awaiting an **official apology** addressed to the Klingon High Command. I expect you to assume full responsibility for the **persecution** of Klingon nationals in this quadrant.

An apology? You are expecting **me** to make an official apology?

I rather doubt if the Klingons could have thought of a more **inauspicious** moment to voice their complaint.

Yes! You have harassed my men. You have treated them like criminals. You've been most uncourteous, Captain Kirk. Now, if you wish to avoid a diplomatic incident--
No, Kirk. You can't let him. That will give the Klingons the wedge they need to claim Sherman's Planet.
I believe that more than the word of an aggrieved Klingon commandeer would be necessary for that, Mr. Baris.

Mr. Spock, as far as Sherman's Planet is concerned, Captain Kirk has **already** given it to us.

Well, we'll see about **that.** But before I take any official action, I'd like to know just what happened.

As the tribbles are carried out of the room they pass Baris' assistant Darvin and something **very strange** happens.

Hey, what's the matter with these things?

SCREEEEECH!!!!
SCREEEEECH!!!!

Get those things away from me!

Remarkable.

Hold on a minute!

Kirk takes two tribbles in his hands and they begin to purr. But as he nears the Klingon officers, the tribbles start to shake and squeak violently!
SCREECH!!! SCREECH!!!
Why, you're **right,** Mr. Jones. They **don't** like Klingons.
SCREECH!!! SCREECH!!!
Next, Kirk moves to Spock and the tribbles relax.
Hmmm. . . But they **do** like **Vulcans.** Why, Mr. Spock, I didn't know you had it in you.
Obviously tribbles are **very perceptive** creatures, Captain.
purrrr purrrr

Continuing his experiment, Kirk approaches the Under-Secretary.
Mr. Baris, they like **you.** Well. . .there's no accounting for taste.
purrrr purrrr
Finally he returns to Darvin and once again the tribbles become extremely agitated.
But they don't like **you,** Mr. Darvin. I wonder why?
SCREEECH!!!!! SCREEEECH!!!!!

SCREEECH!!!! SCREEEEECH!!!!
Ah, Dr. McCoy. We seem to have a rather **unusual** situation here. Would you run your scanner over Mr. Darvin?
Certainly, Captain.
The results are both startling and revealing.
This is quite strange. His **heartbeat** is all wrong. His **body temperature** is--
Jim! This man is a **Klingon.**

A Klingon? You must be mistaken!

I wonder what Star Fleet Command will say about this? Bones, what about the grain?
Oh, yes. It was poisoned!
Poisoned?
Yes, poisoned. It's been impregnated with a virus that turns into an inert material in the blood stream. The more an organism eats, the more inert matter is built up. So, in this case, after two or three days, it reached a point where the tribbles couldn't take in enough nourishment to survive.

You mean they **starved** to death? In a storage compartment full of grain, they starved to death?
That is essentially it.
Determined to get to the bottom of the whole situation, Kirk returns to Darvin. The tribbles again start up with their noises and try desperately to jump out of Kirk's hands and get at the Klingon.
SCREECH!!! SCREEEEECH!!!
Now then, are you going to talk to **me** or, perhaps, you'd rather have a chat with these little **tribbles.**

All right! I'll talk. I poisoned the grain. Just take them away!

Then the tribbles had **nothing** to do with it?

I don't know. I never saw one before in my life. And I hope I **never** see one of those fuzzy miserable things again!

I'm **certain** that can be arranged. Guards, take this man away.

With one Klingon taken care of, Kirk turns his attention to the others.

Captain Koloth, I believe you were saying something about an **apology?** Well, there's no need...and **no time.** I'm giving you **exactly** six hours to get your ship **out** of Federation territory. **Have a safe journey!**

As the Klingons leave the space station and Baris is occupied interrogating Darvin, Kirk can at last relax.

You know, McCoy, I think I could learn to **like** these tribbles.
Sometimes the Captain acts **too much** like a human.
prrrr prrrrrr

Well, my **dear** Captain Kirk, I guess I'll be going on my way now.
I think not, my **dear** Mr. Jones. There is a **slight matter** I wish to discuss with you. Will you please follow me?

Kirk and Spock and Cyrano make their way to the space station's bar.
Why, how **kind** of you, Captain. A farewell drink?
Not exactly. I wanted to show you something. Here, take a look. What do you see?

Nothing much. Just the bartender and . . . eh . . . a few little tribbles.

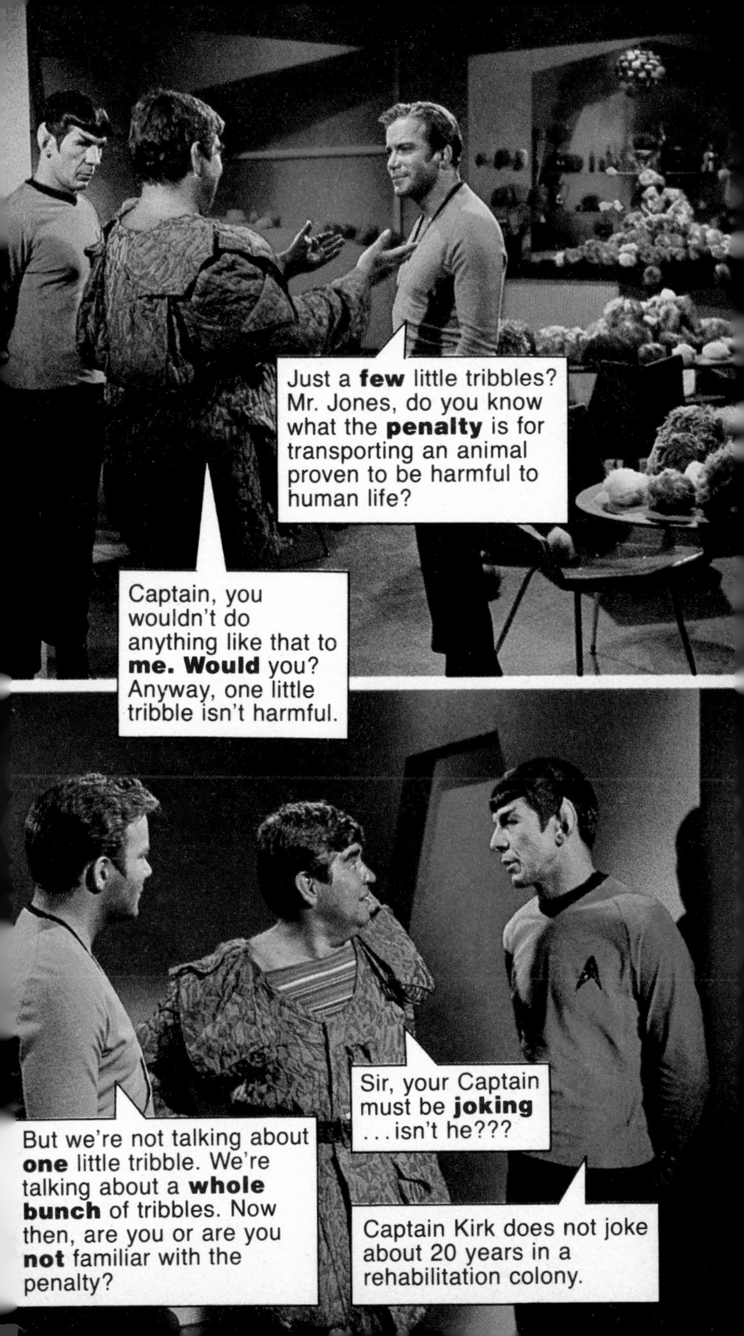
Just a **few** little tribbles? Mr. Jones, do you know what the **penalty** is for transporting an animal proven to be harmful to human life?
Captain, you wouldn't do anything like that to **me. Would** you? Anyway, one little tribble isn't harmful.
But we're not talking about **one** little tribble. We're talking about a **whole bunch** of tribbles. Now then, are you or are you **not** familiar with the penalty?
Sir, your Captain must be **joking** ...isn't he???
Captain Kirk does not joke about 20 years in a rehabilitation colony.

Captain Kirk . . . **friend** . . . Surely we can come to some sort of **mutual understanding.**
After all, my tribbles **did** put you wise to the poisoned grain and they **did** help you find the Klingon agent. We saved a lot of **lives** that way. You **can't** just forget **that,** can you?

No, I can't. That is why I am going to do you a favor. If you pick up **every** tribble on the space station, I'll speak to Mr. Lurry about returning your space ship.

But that would take **years**!

17.9, to be exact.

Like the proverbial thousand mile journey that begins with one step, Cyrano begins.

My dear friend, this work is quite tiring. Perhaps you would be so kind as to pour me a **small refreshment.**

You must be **kidding.** There isn't a **drop** left of **anything.** The tribbles finished me off this afternoon.

The U.S.S. Enterprise gracefully pulls away from the space station and moves out into the far reaches of the galaxy as its crew readies itself for its next mission...

...and Kirk returns to his responsibilities as a Starship Captain.

Captain, Star Fleet was able to divert that freighter.

Good! That means Sherman's Planet will get its quadro-triticale only a few weeks late.

Settling into his chair, something catches his eye—or rather, the **lack** of something catches his eye.

What happened? I don't see **any** tribbles around here. Bones! How'd you **do** that?

Well, I can't take credit for another man's work. **Scotty** did it.

Scotty! **Good work!** Where are the tribbles?

Uh... Captain, it was really **Mr. Spock's** recommendation.

I see. Well then, Mr. Spock, where are all the tribbles?
Based on computer analysis, of course, and taking into account all possibilities and relying on **Dr. McCoy's** input I--
Gentlemen, I don't want to interrupt this . . . eh . . . **mutual admiration society,** but I'd **like** to know **where** the tribbles are.
I'd really like to be the one to tell you, but it was **Mr. Scott** who performed the actual engineering.

Captain Kirk! That would be inhuman.
I could never do such a thing. I gave them a very good home. I gave them to the Klingons.
You gave them to the Klingons???
Aye, sir. Before they went into warp, I transported the whole kit and kaboodle into their engine room where they'll be no "tribble" at all!
HA HA
HEE HEE
HO HO
HA HA HA

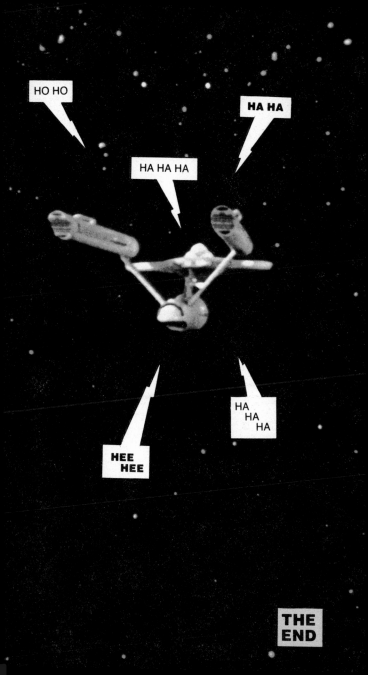

GLOSSARY

Bridge—The top deck of the Starship from which the Captain, his chief officers, and the navigator control the ship.

Communicator—Portable piece of equipment the size of a package of cigarettes, used primarily for maintaining communication between landing parties on the surface of a planet and the orbiting spaceship.

Credit—Monetary unit used and accepted throughout the Federation of Planets.

Donatu V—The site of an inconclusive battle between the Federation and the Klingon Empire.

Klingons—The chief enemies of the Federation. Though brutal and aggressive by nature, they are also extremely efficient in achieving their aims.

Medical Scanner—A portable sensor usually carried by Dr. McCoy when away from Sickbay, capable of sensing, analysing and supplying information concerning the medical condition of the being under examination.

Parsec—A unit of measure for interstellar space equal to 3.26 light years.

Sherman's Planet—An undeveloped planet located near deep space station K-7 that is claimed by both the Federation and the Klingons.

Ship's Log—Record keeping method used by the Captain of all activities aboard the Starship.

Sickbay—The area of the Starship where all major medical procedures are performed.

Stardate—Method of calculating time on board the Starship.

Star Fleet Command—Main headquarters for all space ship communications.

Transporter—Used to move crew and/or cargo from the Starship to planets and back by changing the object's original molecular structure into energy which is beamed to a predetermined point where the original molecular formation is reconstructed.

Tribble—Extremely affectionate oval creatures measuring approximately three to seven inches in length, capable of reproducing every 12 hours.

United Federation of Planets—Democratic alliance of planets comprised of several solar systems, including Sol. All decisions affecting member planets are made through delegates to the Federation Council.

U.S.S. *Enterprise*—One of 13 starships with a crew of approximately 430. Its 11 decks contain a completely self-supporting mini-city.

Viewscreen—Electronic devices located throughout the ship that put crew members in visual contact with all other areas of the ship.

Vulcans—Race inhabiting the planet Vulcan, recognizable by their highly developed intelligence, pointed ears, upswept eyebrows and sallow complexion. Their lives are ruled primarily by logic, not emotion.

STAR TREK QUIZ #3

In each question, circle the one answer that *best* completes the sentence.

1. Quadro-triticale is:

   a. a small furry creature
   b. a 4-lobed perennial
   c. a high-yield hybrid of wheat and alfalfa
   d. the only plant life that is capable of growing on space station K-7.

2. The *Enterprise*'s crew gets into a fight with the Klingons when they:

   a. insult Captain Kirk
   b. pick on Chekov
   c. criticize the Starship
   d. try to poison the quadro-triticale

3. A tribble has a remarkable ability to:

   a. add
   b. subtract
   c. multiply
   d. divide

4. Cyrano Jones is a:

   a. bartender
   b. licensed asteroid prospector
   c. Klingon spy
   d. native of K-7

5. One use of Antarian Glow Water is as:

   a. a polisher for flame gems
   b. an after dinner drink
   c. a perfume
   d. a decay preventative

6. The Organian Peace Treaty concerns:

a. space station K-7
b. Donatu V
c. Deneb IV
d. Sherman's Planet

7. A priority-one distress call signifies:

a. a disaster
b. an approaching alien spaceship
c. radiation activity
d. insufficient food supplies

8. Nilz Baris' major responsibility is:

a. inter-galactic foreign policy affairs
b. security on Space Station K-7
c. arranging a peace treaty between the Klingons and the United Federation
d. the Agricultural Development Project for Sherman's Planet

9. Arne Darvin is:

a. a spy from Sherman's Planet
b. Lurry's assistant
c. a Klingon
d. an android

10. The tribbles died because:

a. Scott transported them to the Klingon ship
b. the quadro-triticale was poisoned
c. they suffocated in the storage bins
d. their life span was shortened by their exposure to the Klingons

Turn the page for the answers.

Forced to land on the unfriendly planet Eminiar VII by an over-zealous Federation Ambassador, Captain Kirk and Spock find themselves and their Starship **unwilling participants** in what at first appears to be a ridiculous and senseless game.

The Eminians are at war with their neighboring planet Vendikar. But it is a war **unlike** any other. For it is not fought by people with guns, but rather by people with **computers.** Battles are programmed, attacks are mathematically launched and deaths are calculated.

To Kirk it is a foolish game, one which he refuses to play. But he is given **no choice.** The Eminians are **deadly** serious and the point is dramatically driven home when Kirk is informed that the Vendikans' computer has considered the **U.S.S.** *Enterprise* a legitimate target and has classified it **"destroyed."**

NO! This is definitely NOT a game!

Kirk and Spock have just one day to try to stop a war that has been waging for 500 years, or they will get much more than...

A TASTE OF ARMAGEDDON

COMING SOON,
wherever paperback books are sold.

ANSWERS to Quiz on preceding pages.

1.**b**   2.**c**   3.**c**   4.**b**   5.**a**   6.**d**   7.**a**   8.**d**   9.**c**   10.**b**

THE EXCITING REALM OF STAR TREK